ENG

MW01201306

WORD

EXERCISES

(PART 1)

FILL IN THE BLANKS

MANIK JOSHI

<u>Dedication</u>

THIS BOOK IS

DEDICATED

TO THOSE

WHO REALIZE

THE POWER OF ENGLISH

AND WANT TO

LEARN IT

SINCERELY

Copyright Notice

All rights reserved. Please note that the content in this book is protected under copyright law. This book is for your personal use only. No part of this book may be reproduced, stored in a retrieval system, or transmitted, in any form or by any means, electronic, mechanical, recording, or otherwise, without the prior written permission of the author.

Copyright Holder -- Manik Joshi
License -- Standard Copyright License
Year of Publication -- 2015
Email -- manik85joshi@gmail.com

****

IMPORTANT NOTE

This Book is Part of a Series
SERIES Name: "English Worksheets"
[A Ten-Book Series]
BOOK Number: 01
BOOK Title: "English Word Exercises (Part 1)"
****

Table of Contents

Fill In the Blanks – 01 - 20

(Exercise 01)

01. Decision to expel them has put the lives of their kids in **j _ _ _ _ _ _ y.**

02. He dismissed **s _ _ _ _ _ _ _ _ _ _ s** about his political ambitions.

03. He forced the Board to **a _ _ _ _ _ n** its working committee meeting last week.

04. She rushed to the spot after hearing the **s _ _ _ _ _ _ _ _ g** of car wheels and the commotion.

05. Intelligence agencies had failed to gauge the **m _ _ _ _ _ _ _ e** of the crisis and did not act in time.

06. It requires a lot of hard work to **c _ _ _ _ _ _ _ e** flowers since they have a limited shelf-life.

07. O _ _ _ _ _ _ _ n of women is a universal issue that has nothing to do with a certain nationality.

08. Protestors have agreed not to **e _ _ _ _ _ _ e** their agitation for the next 10 days.

09. Rainfall continued in many parts for the second **c _ _ _ _ _ _ _ _ _ e** day.

10. Roof of her house had weakened by the recent spate of **i _ _ _ _ _ _ _ t** rainfall.

11. Several appeals are pending and many convicts are **l _ _ _ _ _ _ _ _ _ g** in jails.

12. Several localities received electricity for only a few hours and were **p _ _ _ _ _ d** into darkness for the most part of the night.

13. Suddenly the tables started **t _ _ _ _ _ _ _ g** and paintings on the wall fell on the ground.

14. Tenders will be **f _ _ _ _ _ d** soon so that companies may be allotted the work by the next month-end.

15. The prices of vegetables shot up **e _ _ _ _ _ _ _ _ _ _ y** in the recent past.

16. Their **g _ _ _ _ _ _ _ _ s** are being addressed by officials concerned.

17. There is a need to **t _ _ _ _ _ _ _ m** all the negativity into positivity.

18. Water-logging caused many low-lying areas to be **s _ _ _ _ _ _ _ d** underwater, leading to traffic snarls.

19. We believe funds should be **d _ _ _ _ _ _ _ d** among those who really need it.

20. Wet and chilly weather **h _ _ _ _ _ _ d** relief work.

ANSWERS

01. jeopardy | 02. speculations | 03. abandon | 04. screeching | 05. magnitude | 06. cultivate | 07. oppression | 08. escalate | 09. consecutive | 10. incessant | 11. languishing | 12. plunged | 13. trembling | 14. floated | 15. exorbitantly | 16. grievances | 17. transform | 18. submerged | 19. disbursed | 20. hampered

Fill In the Blanks – 21 - 40
(Exercise 02)

21. A powerful earthquake **t _ _ _ _ _ d** a tower in the city.

22. An employee saw smoke **b _ _ _ _ _ _ _ g** out of the building.

23. Children said they saw the leopard passing through dense **f** _ _ _ _ _ **e.**

24. Every person has the right to practice his faith without any **p** _ _ _ _ _ _ _ _ _ **n.**

25. Fire officials **s** _ _ _ _ _ _ _ **d** short circuit to be the cause of this incident.

26. He was taken to the hospital and **d** _ _ _ _ _ _ _ _ **d** after providing first aid.

27. Hospitals have been **s** _ _ _ _ _ **d** with sufficient amounts of the medicines.

28. Many localities faced long **u** _ _ _ _ _ _ _ _ _ **d** power cuts.

29. **N_** _ _ _ _ _ **d** in the midst of lush green mounds, this museum is a storehouse of knowledge.

30. One thousand patients have been **a** _ _ _ _ _ _ _ _ _ _ _ **d** with the vaccine.

31. Our country must develop fast to meet the **a** _ _ _ _ _ _ _ _ _ **s** of the people.

32. Our state has **t** _ _ _ _ _ _ _ _ **s** potential in the field of tourism.

33. Rainfall will **r** _ _ _ _ _ _ _ **h** water reserves by increasing groundwater tables.

34. The department of ancient history will carry out an **e** _ _ _ _ _ _ _ _ **n** in the village.

35. The swelling river had **i** _ _ _ _ _ _ _ **d** nearly 200 acres of agricultural land.

36. There was a **w** _ _ _ _ _ **r** in the social media about the opening of a new university.

37. There was a slight problem at the platform, which was **r _ _ _ _ _ _ _ d** by the engineering team soon after the information was passed on by the station master.

38. They come from different faiths and **c _ _ _ _ _ _ _ e** Hindu, Muslim and Christian festivals in the same spirit.

39. They failed to **g _ _ _ e** the depth of the river and died.

40. Why can't we make quality electronic goods that are globally **c _ _ _ _ _ _ _ _ _ e?**

ANSWERS

21. toppled | 22. billowing | 23. foliage | 24. persecution | 25. suspected | 26. discharged | 27. stocked | 28. unscheduled | 29. nestled | 30. administered | 31. aspirations | 32. tremendous | 33. replenish | 34. excavation | 35. inundated | 36. whisper | 37. rectified | 38. celebrate | 39. gauge | 40. competitive

Fill In the Blanks – 41 - 60
(Exercise 03)

41. A rhinoceros was **m _ _ _ _ _ _ _ d** by poachers for its horn.

42. Assailants faced no **r _ _ _ _ _ _ _ _ e** and fled on their bikes.

43. Bank officials threatened him of **c _ _ _ _ _ _ e** action if he failed to repay the loan.

44. Business chambers **p _ _ _ _ d** the loss to the economy at a staggering one billion dollar.

45. The government has **e _ _ _ _ _ _ _ d** an amount of 1 billion dollars for the project.

46. Farmers' hopes of a bumper crop were dashed by the rain, leaving them facing a **b _ _ _ k** future.

47. He had complained of chest pain following which he **f _ _ _ _ _ d.**

48. His support to his investigation seems to have **b _ _ _ _ _ _ _ d.**

49. Hunters **l _ _ _ _ d** the skill to shoot the thick-skinned animal.

50. China was **r _ _ _ _ d** 62 among 189 countries last year.

51. Officer has directed them to conduct the work in a prompt and **t _ _ _ _ _ _ _ _ _ t** manner.

52. Officials visited the plant site and held **d _ _ _ _ _ _ _ _ _ _ _ s** on the project.

53. Our armed forces stand fully capable to deal with all sorts of external **a _ _ _ _ _ _ _ _ n.**

54. Pilgrims **s _ _ _ _ _ _ d** after rains caused massive landslides and washed away bridges along the routes.

55. The bench said the convicts will have to undergo the punishment without any **r _ _ _ _ _ _ _ n.**

56. The CM was in the city to **i _ _ _ _ _ _ _ _ e** an oil mill at a private function.

57. The official also warned legal action against him for his **s _ _ _ _ _ _ _ _ s** campaign.

58. The teachers are demanding payment of **o _ _ _ _ _ _ _ _ _ g** dues of previous years evaluation work.

59. They feared that the dead people's spirits would **p _ _ _ _ _ s** them.

60. This was suspected to be a tour to **e _ _ _ _ _ e** ancient city.

ANSWERS

41. mutilated | 42. resistance | 43. coercive | 44. pegged | 45. earmarked | 46. bleak | 47. fainted | 48. backfired | 49. lacked | 50. ranked | 51. transparent | 52. deliberations | 53. aggression | 54. stranded | 55. remission | 56. inaugurate | 57. slanderous | 58. outstanding | 59. possess | 60. explore

Fill In the Blanks – 61 - 80
(Exercise 04)

61. An agreement was reached between the district administration and the **a _ _ _ _ _ _ _ d** families.

62. Ensure peace and **h _ _ _ _ _ y** in the entire state.

63. The government was making efforts to have air route open to **r _ _ _ _ e** its nationals from the city.

64. He was **g _ _ _ _ _ _ s** in his praise of president who he has immense respect for.

65. A large number of people converged to get a last **g _ _ _ _ _ e** of the departed leader.

66. Little had they **e _ _ _ _ _ _ d** to find empty roads and home shut from outside.

67. My thoughts and prayers are with the families of the **d** _ _ _ _ _ _ **d** in this hour of grief.

68. Nobody having black money will be **s** _ _ _ _ **d**.

69. NSA-level talks scheduled between the two countries amid **a** _ _ _ _ _ _ **y**.

70. Our company **i** _ _ _ _ _ _ **d** revenue losses in excess of 10 million dollars.

71. Police was trying to shield the accused by **t** _ _ _ _ _ _ _ **g** with the evidence.

72. Rival parties arrived at the spot and **i**_ _ _ _ _ _ **d** in heavy brick-batting.

73. Senior citizens are well-off with most having children **s** _ _ _ _ _ **d** abroad.

74. Several political groups held a massive **d** _ _ _ _ _ _ _ _ _ _ **n** on Tuesday morning.

75. Some protestors forced taxi drivers off the roads and **v** _ _ _ _ _ _ _ **d** their vehicles.

76. The kingpin of the gang, a man has so far **e** _ _ _ _ **d** arrest.

77. The use of unfair means is not just **p** _ _ _ _ _ _ _ **t** in academic examinations but also for securing a driving license.

78. This is the first such incident I have **w** _ _ _ _ _ _ _ **d** in my entire career.

79. Vehicle **b** _ _ _ _ **d** into a truck after going on the wrong side.

80. We **o** _ _ _ _ _ **d** floral tributes and lit candles at the memorial.

ANSWERS

61. aggrieved | 62. harmony | 63. rescue | 64. generous | 65. glimpse | 66. expected | 67. deceased | 68. spared | 69. acrimony | 70. incurred | 71. tampering | 72. indulged | 73. settled | 74. demonstration | 75. vandalized | 76. evaded | 77. prevalent | 78. witnessed | 79. bumped | 80. offered

Fill In the Blanks – 81 - 100
(Exercise 05)

81. A four-foot-tall statue of the leader has been **e _ _ _ _ _ d**.

82. Airline has **c _ _ _ _ _ _ _ _ _ d** a three-member panel to go into the pros and cons of the proposal.

83. Cops **m _ _ _ _ _ _ _ _ d** those protesting quietly.

84. Do they not want the reservation system to be **a _ _ _ _ _ _ _ d**?

85. He arrived at the spot to express **s _ _ _ _ _ _ _ _ y** with the protestors.

86. He died while **u _ _ _ _ _ _ _ _ g** treatment.

87. He has been **d _ _ _ _ _ d** on the basis of his mobile phone location.

88. His eyes were **b _ _ _ _ _ _ g** with tears.

89. Pause, look for trains, and then **p _ _ _ _ _ d**.

90. People have started **v _ _ _ _ _ g** their doubts.

91. The audience started **t _ _ _ _ _ _ g** out.

92. The condition of most of these parks is **p _ _ _ _ _ _ c**.

93. The sound of gunshots left local residents **s _ _ _ _ _ _ _ g** for cover.

94. They are advised by travel agents not to **i _ _ _ _ _ _ t** with the locals, as they may be duped.

95. They do not know how old this **t _ _ _ _ _ _ _ n** is.

96. They have been asked to drop all such projects and **f _ _ _ _ e** funds for them.

97. They were accused of creating a **n _ _ _ _ _ _ e** and assaulting fellow passengers.

98. Three suspected thieves were allegedly **l _ _ _ _ _ d** by a mob.

99. We do not want to create **r _ _ _ _ _ _ _ _ s** in the path of the nation's progress.

100. We have sent several **r _ _ _ _ _ _ _ s** to the seniors but are yet to receive a reply.

ANSWERS

81. erected | 82. constituted | 83. manhandled | 84. abolished | 85. solidarity | 86. undergoing | 87. detained | 88. brimming | 89. proceed | 90. voicing | 91. thinning | 92. pathetic | 93. scurrying | 94. interact | 95. tradition | 96. freeze | 97. nuisance | 98. lynched | 99. roadblocks | 100. reminders

Fill In the Blanks – 101 - 120
(Exercise 06)

101. Austria **w _ _ _ _ _ w** its ambassador in protest of the incident.

102. He was **c _ _ _ _ _ e** since being hospitalized.

103. He was s _ _ _ _ _ d by miscreants who place a handkerchief over her face.

104. His love for that girl went u _ _ _ _ _ _ _ _ d.

105. I have no i _ _ _ _ _ _ _ n of hiding who I am.

106. It was hard to even a _ _ _ _ s what the extent of damage around the city could be.

107. Our school doesn't have a big hall to a _ _ _ _ _ _ _ _ e students.

108. Police took prompt steps to t _ _ _ _ e the situation.

109. Rebels fought f _ _ _ _ _ _ y.

110. River's water r _ _ _ _ _ _ d muddy and at knee level.

111. S _ _ _ _ _ _ g train hit them while they were crossing the railway tracks at an unmanned level crossing.

112. The sessions court had passed an order staying the d _ _ _ _ _ _ _ _ n.

113. Several shops were g _ _ _ _ d after a fire broke out inside a garment market.

114. The breakdown of talks has d _ _ _ _ _ _ d the crisis.

115. The decision was taken at the party's parliamentary board meeting p _ _ _ _ _ _ d over by the party chief.

116. The protestors demanded shifting of the garbage ground from their locality to the o _ _ _ _ _ _ _ s of the city.

117. The seven parties have m _ _ _ _ d to form a new party.

118. There is a growing demand for e _ _ _ _ _ _ _ e unmanned railway crossing across the state.

119. There were thousands of buildings with structural v _ _ _ _ _ _ _ _ s in the city.

120. This case b _ _ _ _ _ t back the horror of the last year's fire incident.

ANSWERS

101. withdrew | 102. comatose | 103. sedated | 104. unrequited | 105. intention | 106. assess | 107. accommodate | 108. tackle | 109. fiercely | 110. remained | 111. speeding | 112. demolition | 113. gutted | 114. deepened | 115. presided | 116. outskirts | 117. merged | 118. eliminate | 119. violations | 120. brought

Fill In the Blanks – 121 - 140
(Exercise 07)

121. A mail **p _ _ _ _ d** up in his inbox.

122. Auction **f _ _ _ _ _ d** about $ 1 million.

123. Authority **r _ _ _ _ _ _ _ _ _ d** that the number 150 be adopted as the single emergency number.

124. Bus tried to run over him but a **v_ _ _ _ _ _ _ r** pushed him to safety.

125. Emailed queries in this regard remained **u _ _ _ _ _ _ _ d**.

126. Footage posted online showed helicopters **h _ _ _ _ _ _ g** over the site of the blaze.

127. Forest staff caught three poachers who were attempting to kill a deer by **e _ _ _ _ _ _ _ _ t**.

128. He greeted him with a **s _ _ _ _ _ _ _ _ _ s** hug.

129. He has been **b _ _ _ _ _ _ g** ill health.

130. He is known for **o _ _ _ _ _ _ _ _ h** claims about its own prowess.

131. He is s _ _ _ _ _ _ _ e about almost everything it does.

132. He t _ _ _ _ _ _ d a written apology to the college administration.

133. He was m _ _ _ _ d and drawn into a conspiracy.

134. His p _ _ _ _ _ _ _ _ n seems to have some basis.

135. Politics must be c _ _ _ _ _ _ d of criminal elements.

136. Such a petty issue has reached an a _ _ _ _ _ _ g proportion, which is affecting the daily lives of many employees.

137. They were bowled over by her j _ _ _ _ l nature and affection towards elderly people.

138. They were i _ _ _ _ _ _ _ _ _ _ e after their defeat.

139. Three new cabinet ministers were on s _ _ _ n in to the new national government.

140. We were promised flats long back but that never c _ _ _ _ _ _ _ _ d into reality.

ANSWERS

121. popped | **122.** fetched | **123.** recommend | **124.** volunteer | **125.** unanswered | **126.** hovering | **127.** entrapment | **128.** spontaneous | **129.** battling | **130.** outlandish | **131.** secretive | **132.** tendered | **133.** misled | **134.** perception | **135.** cleansed | **136.** alarming | **137.** jovial | **138.** inconsolable | **139.** sworn | **140.** culminated

Fill In the Blanks – 141 - 160
(Exercise 08)

141. Aircraft remained **a _ _ _ _ _ _ e** for almost twenty minutes before landing back at the airport.

142. All **e _ _ _ _ _ _ g** challenges will be suitably addressed.

143. Complainants **p _ _ _ _ d** in of large scale corruption in the payrolls.

144. The driver should remain calm and focused which helps reduce road **m _ _ _ _ _ s.**

145. F_ _ _ _ _ g that the issue might become too big to handle, hospital staff rushed to control the damage.

146. He **g _ _ _ _ _ _ d** 1 million 'likes' on social networking sites.

147. I am shocked that my name **d _ _ _ _ _ d** into this matter.

148. No one will be allowed to violate the law and **s _ _ _ _ _ _ _ t** action will be taken against them.

149. Passersby found an unclaimed suitcase on a scooter **p _ _ _ _ d** in front of one of the banks.

150. PM **c _ _ _ _ _ _ d** a high-level meeting to take stock of the situation.

151. Police had to call for **r _ _ _ _ _ _ _ _ _ _ _ t** to quell the agitation.

152. The helpline was **l _ _ _ _ _ _ d** in November 2014.

153. The issue of national security cannot be **c _ _ _ _ _ _ _ _ _ d.**

154. The locals **b _ _ _ _ _ d** the tracks and refused to allow the special train.

155. The miscreants kept them captive for around an hour and **d _ _ _ _ _ _ d** with cash and valuables.

156. The **q _ _ _ _ _ m** of punishment will be pronounced on Monday.

157. The **s _ _ _ _ _ g** (due to earthquake) was so severe that I couldn't even stand.

158. They **i _ _ _ _ _ d** people present there.

159. They **s _ _ _ t** open the pods to remove the white or purple cocoa beans.

160. Two accomplices opened fire and police fired back in **r _ _ _ _ _ _ _ _ _ n**.

ANSWERS

141. airborne | 142. emerging | 143. poured | 144. mishaps | 145. fearing | 146. garnered | 147. dragged | 148. stringent | 149. parked | 150. convened | 151. reinforcement | 152. launched | 153. compromised | 154. blocked | 155. decamped | 156. quantum | 157. shaking | 158. incited | 159. split | 160. retaliation

Fill In the Blanks – 161 - 180
(Exercise 09)

161. Army **r _ _ _ _ _ _ _ d** hundreds of soldiers who were dismissed for alleged indiscipline in the battle.

162. Batsman **s _ _ _ _ d** the bowlers to all parts of the ground.

163. He had expressed his desire that his body be **d _ _ _ _ _ d** to the medical university.

164. He was trying to create **r _ _ t** between us.

165. He is trying to **d _ _ _ _ n** the people of our country.

166. I don't see an environment where credit growth is **t _ _ _ d**.

167. Leaders agreed to strengthen **c** _ _ _ _ _ _ _ _ _ _ **n** between the two governments.

168. Liberty sans privacy might be **i** _ _ _ _ _ _ **y**.

169. Local governments have sometimes been **a** _ _ _ _ _ _ _ _ **y** in dealing with this issue.

170. The orientation session was going on at the **c** _ _ _ _ _ _ _ _ _ **n** hall.

171. The road was under repair and stones lay **s** _ _ _ _ _ _ _ **d** all over the place.

172. Seasonal rain and hailstorm **l** _ _ _ _ **d** the region in the first week of March.

173. Security forces **s** _ _ _ _ _ **d** down on the city to oversee security arrangements for the PM's visit.

174. The security situation is more complex and **n** _ _ _ _ _ **d** than earlier and called for round-the-clock vigilance.

175. She fainted in the courtroom as the public prosecutor argued that her custody be further **e** _ _ _ _ _ _ **d**.

176. She said the continuing tremors made the situation rather **p** _ _ _ _ _ _ _ _ **s** near the glaciers.

177. Superstars **o** _ _ _ _ _ **d** residents by visiting their houses and interacting with them.

178. The fear in eyes of villagers was **p** _ _ _ _ _ _ **e**.

179. They celebrated Independence Day with **g** _ _ _ _ **y** and fervor.

180. Today is the last day of **e** _ _ _ _ _ _ _ _ _ _ _ _ **g**.

ANSWERS

161. reinstated | 162. spanked | 163. donated | 164. rift | 165. demean | 166. tepid | 167. collaboration | 168. illusory | 169. arbitrary | 170. convocation | 171. scattered | 172. lashed | 173. swooped | 174. nuanced | 175. extended | 176. precarious | 177. obliged | 178. palpable | 179. gaiety | 180. electioneering

Fill In the Blanks – 181 - 200
(Exercise 10)

181. The army was called in to help control widespread violence s _ _ _ _ _ d by the statehood agitation.

182. As everything is now online, the forgery was d _ _ _ _ _ _ d easily.

183. C _ _ _ _ _ _ g whip on illegal mining, the DM imposed heavy fine to companies for mining.

184. Country g _ _ _ _ _ _ d with fresh floods caused by untimely rain.

185. He allegedly a _ _ _ _ _ d properties disproportionate to their known sources of income.

186. He s _ _ _ _ d a claim on the property.

187. He was q _ _ _ _ _ d late last night by the police.

188. Her body was recovered from the drain after three hours of d _ _ _ _ _ g.

189. If we are served with a court order within the j _ _ _ _ _ _ _ _ _ _ n of the country, we will respond to that.

190. Investigators are yet to reach a definite c _ _ _ _ _ _ _ _ _ s on the motive of the murder.

191. The principal conducted a meeting with teachers to **r _ _ _ _ e** the issue.

192. The prosecution failed to **e _ _ _ _ _ _ h** its case.

193. Rain-swollen rivers **b _ _ _ t** their banks.

194. Our government is **s _ _ _ _ _ g** to reduce the dependence on imports.

195. The incident is suspected to be **f _ _ _ _ t** of the land dispute.

196. The woman **p _ _ _ _ _ _ _ _ d** on the court for claims from her husband.

197. There is nothing wrong with taking up **m _ _ _ _ l** work.

198. This is not a city that can be **i _ _ _ _ _ d**.

199. We **n _ _ _ _ d** the accused at the spot and brought them to the police station.

200. Witnesses **r _ _ _ _ _ d** from their earlier statements.

ANSWERS

181. sparked | 182. detected | 183. cracking | 184. grappled | 185. amassed | 186. staked | 187. quizzed | 188. dredging | 189. jurisdiction | 190. conclusions | 191. resolve | 192. establish | 193. burst | 194. seeking | 195. fallout | 196. petitioned | 197. menial | 198. ignored | 199. nabbed | 200. reneged

Fill In the Blanks – 201 - 220
(Exercise 11)

201. A minor altercation between some people **s** _ _ _ _ _ _ _ **d** into a communal clash.

202. After a **p** _ _ _ _ _ _ _ _ **y** examination, cops suspect that he was kidnapped.

203. Corporation decided to **r** _ _ _ _ _ _ **e** and beautify 10 city parks with a budget of 1 million dollars.

204. Despite getting a befitting reply many times, it is not **m** _ _ _ _ _ **g** his ways.

205. He couldn't believe what he read and **r** _ _ _ _ **d** his eyes and looked again.

206. He must apologize for his **d** _ _ _ _ _ _ _ _ **e** comments.

207. His dead body was **d** _ _ _ _ _ _ _ **d** and covered with flies after six days in the rubble.

208. I thank the people of this country for **s** _ _ _ _ _ _ _ **g** love on me for so long.

209. Lack of manpower and latest equipment makes it difficult for them to deal with fire **h** _ _ _ _ _ **s** across the city.

210. Our country is yet to **c** _ _ _ _ _ _ _ _ **e** on this mode of tourism.

211. Police **g** _ _ _ _ **d** control of the situation after using force.

212. Serious differences appear to have **c** _ _ _ _ _ **d** up in the party.

213. She chose not to comment on the **a** _ _ _ _ _ _ _ _ _ **s**.

214. She **l** _ _ _ _ **d** behind in studies after the absence in school.

215. Five teams have made several raids at his known **h** _ _ _ _ _ _ **s** in the past two weeks.

216. The policemen **e** _ _ _ _ _ _ **d** them to court.

217. There have been instances of **i** _ _ _ _ _ _ _ _ **e**, violence and terror.

218. They **s** _ _ _ _ _ _ _ **d** her dream.

219. They were denied submission of a memorandum **p** _ _ _ _ _ _ _ _ **g** to the local civic body to the senior leader.

220. Trains have been **f** _ _ _ _ _ _ _ _ _ **g** people for several decades.

ANSWERS

201. snowballed | 202. preliminary | 203. renovate | 204. mending | 205. rubbed | 206. deplorable | 207. distended | 208. showering | 209. hazards | 210. capitalize | 211. gained | 212. cropped | 213. allegations | 214. lagged | 215. hideouts | 216. escorted | 217. intolerance | 218. shattered | 219. pertaining | 220. fascinating

Fill In the Blanks – 221 - 240
(Exercise 012)

221. A large number of students left their classes **m** _ _ _ _ **y** and joined the protest for the students' union elections.

222. The court had **d** _ _ _ _ _ **d** some sections against him in the case.

223. Electricity lines fell down on the street and remained **u** _ _ _ _ _ _ _ _ **d** for more than two hours in spite of the complaints from residents.

224. He has **s** _ _ _ _ **d** as a witness in court several times.

225. I haven't said anything **p** _ _ _ _ _ _ _ _ _ **e**.

226. Newspaper **c _ _ _ _ _ d** a highly critical article.

227. No one has been able to **p _ _ _ _ _ _ t** the precise area and timing of the temblor.

228. Power officials were left with no **a _ _ _ _ _ _ _ _ _ e** but to cut supply there.

229. The president has called a meeting to **f _ _ _ _ _ _ e** the name, flag and election symbol of the new party.

230. Simply put, she is doing something **d _ _ _ _ _ _ _ _ y** opposite to what ex-DM used to do.

231. Some people take decisions in haste and later **r _ _ _ _ t** and regret.

232. The earthquake shook up everything very **v _ _ _ _ _ _ _ y.**

233. The scope of the investigation will be **w _ _ _ _ _ d.**

234. There has been a **s _ _ _ _ _ _ _ _ g** 33% increase in patients visiting hospitals.

235. There were no **i _ _ _ _ _ _ _ _ _ s** in the court's dismissal of his petition.

236. They are well aware of the **t _ _ _ _ _ _ _ _ y** of the area.

237. They feel that he does not have the **c _ _ _ _ _ _ _ _ _ s** for this role.

238. They had written to the tourism department sharing their **h _ _ _ _ _ _ _ g** experience.

239. Two kids were **s _ _ _ _ _ _ _ _ d** to death after getting locked in their family's car.

240. We have **d _ _ _ _ _ _ d** all our resources for search and rescues.

ANSWERS

221. midway | 222. dropped | 223. unattended | 224. served | 225. provocative | 226. carried | 227. pinpoint | 228. alternative | 229. finalize | 230. diagonally | 231. repent | 232. violently | 233. widened | 234. staggering | 235. infirmities | 236. topography | 237. credentials | 238. harrowing | 239. suffocated | 240. deployed

Fill In the Blanks – 241 - 260
(Exercise 13)

241. A _ _ _ _ _ _ **d** over the delay in the implementation of the scheme, students launched a protest in the city.

242. At least 200 bodies have been **r** _ _ _ _ _ _ _ **d** from the rubble so far.

243. Common **s** _ _ _ _ _ _ **s** of dengue are fever, skin rash, reduced white cells and low platelet count.

244. Don't allow water to **s** _ _ _ _ _ _ **e** in and around your house in coolers.

245. F _ _ _ _ _ _ _ _ _ **y**, our lives are where they have always been.

246. Gunfire and explosions **e** _ _ _ _ **d** across the city.

247. He **i** _ _ _ _ _ _ _ **d** cuts on themselves in protest.

248. He is **s** _ _ _ _ _ _ _ **d** to retire in November this year.

249. He **p** _ _ _ _ _ **d** a torchlight right at her face.

250. He was taken into preventive **d** _ _ _ _ _ _ _ **n** with several of his supporters.

251. M _ _ _ _ **s** of garbage piled up on the street.

252. Major projects will make **h** _ _ _ _ _ **y** soon.

253. Passengers saw flames, heard blasts and smelled **b _ _ _ _ _ g** rubber on the runway.

254. Teachers have **l _ _ _ _ _ _ _ d** the education officers for giving false information.

255. The leopard population has declined by a **w _ _ _ _ _ _ g** 80% over the past 100 years.

256. The proposals running into several pages has been **c _ _ _ _ _ _ _ _ d** to ministries.

257. There was a deafening bang, the windows and cupboards flew open of their own; everything **r _ _ _ _ _ d.**

258. They constantly face a shortage of space due to **o _ _ _ _ _ _ _ _ _ _ g.**

259. They were accused of having **u _ _ _ _ _ _ _ _ _ _ _ d** in exchange for money from illegal bookies.

260. Time and time again, we have seen **v _ _ _ _ _ s** attacks on members of our community.

ANSWERS

241. agitated | 242. retrieved | 243. symptoms | 244. stagnate | 245. financially | 246. echoed | 247. inflicted | 248. scheduled | 249. pointed | 250. detention | 251. mounds | 252. headway | 253. burning | 254. lambasted | 255. whopping | 256. circulated | 257. rattled | 258. overcrowding | 259. underperformed | 260. vicious

Fill In the Blanks – 261 - 280
(Exercise 14)

261. A few people had rent out a portion of their house for **c** _ _ _ _ _ _ _ _ **l** activity.

262. A heated argument occurred, and a brawl **e** _ _ _ _ **d**.

263. A social worker has called for action against officials for failing to check **i** _ _ _ _ _ **l** construction in the city.

264. Any step which can be termed as anti-national cannot be **t** _ _ _ _ _ _ _ **d**.

265. Deeper quakes have more earth to **a** _ _ _ _ **b** the shaking.

266. The football stadium was located within the **p** _ _ _ _ _ _ _ _ **s** of a sugar factory.

267. He broke through to change the **m** _ _ _ _ _ _ **m** of the innings.

268. He gave a **v** _ _ _ **d** account of his last day in office.

269. He was holding a bag **s** _ _ _ _ _ _ **d** from different sides.

270. He was later made one of the prime **w** _ _ _ _ _ _ _ _ **s** in the case.

271. It is obviously wrong to help to **f** _ _ _ _ _ _ **e**.

272. Man **r** _ _ _ _ **d** a hole in the side of the beehive while working on a garden.

273. Rainfall remained **s** _ _ _ _ _ **d** over the past week and is likely to remain so for the next few days.

274. Standing crops were **f** _ _ _ _ _ _ _ **d** by rain and hail.

275. The state government moved a **r** _ _ _ _ _ _ _ _ _ **n** at against the Centre's notification giving absolute powers to Governor.

276. Stray dogs had become **h** _ _ _ _ _ _ _ _ **d** to eating bloody flesh.

277. They did not feel threatened by the **u _ _ _ _ _ _ _ _ _ _ _ d** influx of refugees into their country.

278. They pulled down the **m _ _ _ _ _ _ _ t** structure.

279. They waylaid him at a **d _ _ _ _ _ _ e** spot to exact revenge.

280. Tribunal **s _ _ _ _ _ d** the authorities for not complying with its orders.

ANSWERS

261. commercial | 262. ensued | 263. illegal | 264. tolerated | 265. absorb | 266. precincts | 267. momentum | 268. vivid | 269. stitched | 270. witnesses | 271. fugitive | 272. ripped | 273. subdued | 274. flattened | 275. resolution | 276. habituated | 277. unprecedented | 278. makeshift | 279. desolate | 280. slammed

Fill In the Blanks – 281 - 300
(Exercise 15)

281. A 14-year-old boy was **e _ _ _ _ _ _ _ _ _ _ d** after he stepped on an open wire.

282. A bus **b _ _ _ d** for Beijing fell into a deep gorge.

283. Aid agencies held a first meeting with the government to **c _ _ _ _ _ _ _ _ e** the relief work.

284. Budget of dollar 2 billion has been **s _ _ _ _ _ _ _ _ d** for the project.

285. Discussions cleared the air on three **p _ _ _ _ _ _ g** issues.

286. He demanded that the government thoroughly **i _ _ _ _ _ _ _ _ e** the matter.

287. He went down fighting **g _ _ _ _ _ _ _ y**.

288. He would also help me in household chores even if I asked her to **c _ _ _ _ _ _ _ _ _ e** on studies.

289. His house remained **m _ _ _ _ d** by supporters.

290. Hope for justice seems to be rapidly **f _ _ _ _ g** away in our locality.

291. I had *no* idea what was to **u _ _ _ _ d**.

292. I have been negotiating with the senior officials to **r _ _ _ _ n** the job.

293. I would like to unconditionally **a _ _ _ _ _ _ _ _ e** for any misunderstanding I may have created unintentionally.

294. Investigating Agency **r _ _ _ _ _ _ d** sketches of two suspected terrorists.

295. People on the spot **d _ _ _ _ _ _ _ _ _ y** tried to dig through piles of bricks.

296. Pesticide dealers should be **o _ _ _ _ _ _ d** to the judicious use of pesticides.

297. She was silent for over a week as she had been **t _ _ _ _ _ _ _ d**.

298. The bag he was carrying flew open, and currency notes lay **s _ _ _ _ n** around.

299. The vulture numbers had been **d _ _ _ _ _ _ _ g** for the past decade.

300. Two robbers **s _ _ _ _ _ _ d** her earrings and pushed her off the speeding vehicle, causing fatal injuries.

ANSWERS

281. electrocuted | 282. bound | 283. coordinate | 284. sanctioned | 285. pressing | 286. investigate | 287. gallantly | 288. concentrate | 289. mobbed | 290. fading | 291. unfold | 292. retain | 293. apologize | 294. released | 295. desperately | 296. oriented | 297. threatened | 298. strewn | 299. dwindling | 300. snatched

Fill In the Blanks – 301 - 320
(Exercise 16)

301. A large number of locals are complaining of fever and **r** _ _ _ _ _ **d** symptoms.

302. A low-tension wire **d** _ _ _ _ _ **d** close to the office building.

303. Accused **e** _ _ _ _ _ _ _ **d** relief over the court's ruling.

304. Actual strength of judges in High Court has gone **s** _ _ _ _ _ _ _ _ _ _ _ **y** down as there were 40 judges working out of sanctioned 60 judges.

305. After one night's rain, my ward was **w** _ _ _ _ _ _ _ _ _ **d**.

306. An agreement had been reached on all **c** _ _ _ _ _ _ _ _ _ _ **s** issues between the parties.

307. The center will **p** _ _ _ _ _ _ _ _ **e** land ordinance.

308. CM paid floral **t** _ _ _ _ _ _ **s** to him.

309. He landed in the hospital after being hit in the head by a **r** _ _ _ _ _ _ _ _ _ **g** bullet.

310. It could be a **m** _ _ _ _ **r** of life and death so caution is required.

311. O _ _ _ _ _ _ _ _ _ **g** drains and unconstructed roads added to their woes.

312. Participants at the three-hour-long meeting **a _ _ _ _ _ _ d** the recent global events.

313. People complained of foul smell **e _ _ _ _ _ _ _ g** from water supplied in the taps.

314. Police raided locations tied to **t _ _ _ _ _ d** officer.

315. President lauded the role played by women in various **s _ _ _ _ _ s** of life.

316. She is said to have been a witness to **h _ _ _ _ _ _ _ _ s** in the case.

317. There was no damage to their hotel even as some buildings in the vicinity **c _ _ _ _ _ _ _ d**.

318. Till recently, the stadium wore **d _ _ _ _ _ _ _ _ _ d** look.

319. Troops **i _ _ _ _ _ _ _ _ _ d** shelling on border posts and civilian area.

320. The TV channel was **s _ _ _ _ _ _ d** off all through Friday evening.

ANSWERS

301. related | **302.** dangled | **303.** expressed | **304.** significantly | **305.** waterlogged | **306.** contentious | **307.** promulgate | **308.** tributes | **309.** ricocheting | **310.** matter | **311.** overflowing | **312.** analyzed | **313.** emanating | **314.** tainted | **315.** spheres | **316.** happenings | **317.** collapsed | **318.** dilapidated | **319.** intensified | **320.** switched

Fill In the Blanks – 321 - 340
(Exercise 17)

321. 100 tons of ripe tomatoes were **o _ _ _ _ _ _ d** from seven trucks.

322. A team of the forest department is laying traps to catch the pack of **f _ _ _ l** dogs.

323. An avalanche **u _ _ _ _ _ _ _ d** by the earthquake swept through the base camp.

324. Armed with sticks, rolling pins and brooms, the women **t _ _ _ _ _ _ d** the thief.

325. The city is getting up to 16 hours of power supply and **r _ _ _ _ _ _ g** hours are looked after by senior officials to keep a check on grid frequency.

326. City **s _ _ _ _ _ d** of water, fuel and electricity.

327. The government has not been able to **d _ _ _ _ _ r** on any front, despite being in office for almost a year.

328. He was not sounding in good health and appeared **d _ _ _ _ _ _ _ _ _ _ d** with no ray of hope.

329. Investigating team **p _ _ _ _ d** the case and furnished the findings at the earliest.

330. M _ _ _ _ _ t continued over a wide area of northern France.

331. A pall of gloom **c _ _ _ _ _ _ _ d** to loom over the city.

332. Residents of nearby towers were **e _ _ _ _ _ _ _ d** as helicopters took part in the firefighting operations.

333. The ruling party accused the opposition of creating **o _ _ _ _ _ _ _ s** in the path of economic growth.

334. These irregularities **g _ _ _ _ e** up the opportunity of a genuine candidate.

335. They lifted one of their senior **c _ _ _ _ _ _ _ _ s** on their shoulders.

336. To avoid mosquito bites during day time, wear full-sleeved clothing and apply mosquito **r _ _ _ _ _ _ _ t**.

337. Two of the miscreants were **a** _ _ _ _ _ _ _ _ _ **d** while two others managed to escape.

338. Two policemen were placed under **s** _ _ _ _ _ _ _ _ **n** after they were found guilty of quarreling with two youth.

339. We must ensure that terrorists do not **i** _ _ _ _ _ _ _ _ _ **e** into our territory.

340. Witness **w** _ _ _ _ **d** to remain unnamed.

ANSWERS

321. offloaded | 322. feral | 323. unleashed | 324. thrashed | 325. roasting | 326. starved | 327. deliver | 328. disillusioned | 329. probed | 330. manhunt | 331. continued | 332. evacuated | 333. obstacles | 334. gobble | 335. colleagues | 336. repellent | 337. apprehended | 338. suspension | 339. infiltrate | 340. wished

Fill In the Blanks – 341 - 360
(Exercise 18)

341. A **s** _ _ _ _ _ _ **e** number of cross-sections of people including top officials rushed to his residence.

342. A _ _ _ _ _ **s** people called up their relatives and enquired about their well-being.

343. A magistrate extended the police custody of two accused in the **e** _ _ _ _ _ _ _ **n** case till May 28.

344. Ban was **i** _ _ _ _ _ **d** on the airing of his interview.

345. Cyclone **l** _ _ _ _ **d** the truck from the road and flung it about 100 feet.

346. Storm **s** _ _ _ _ **k** terror in the hearts of panic-stricken residents.

347. He followed her movements through her voice and the **r** _ _ _ _ **e** of fabric.

348. He is believed to have **e** _ _ _ _ **d** the trust of the leader.

349. He played an online computer game for 20 days **s** _ _ _ _ _ _ **t**.

350. He tried hard to keep his eyes from **w** _ _ _ _ _ **g**.

351. I **s** _ _ _ _ _ _ _ _ **e** with the cause.

352. Joblessness is **f** _ _ _ _ _ _ **g** unrest in the country.

353. No relief has been **r** _ _ _ _ _ _ **d** so far.

354. President described the attack as **d** _ _ _ _ _ _ _ _ **e** and cowardly.

355. She can **b** _ _ _ _ **y** speak and can do almost nothing for herself.

356. She is **c** _ _ _ _ _ _ _ _ _ _ _ **g** at home and taking medicine.

357. They had to spend over two years in camps after the **c** _ _ _ _ _ _ _ **l** riots.

358. We have warned villagers from **v** _ _ _ _ _ _ _ _ **g** close to the river due to the presence of crocodiles.

359. We **p** _ _ _ _ **d** in money to hire a lawyer.

360. Wire **s** _ _ _ _ _ **d** and came in contact with the ground.

ANSWERS

341. sizeable | 342. anxious | 343. extortion | 344. imposed | 345. lifted | 346. struck | 347. rustle | 348. earned | 349. straight | 350. welling | 351. sympathize | 352. fuelling | 353. rendered | 354. despicable | 355.

barely | 356. convalescing | 357. communal | 358. venturing | 359. pooled | 360. snapped

Fill In the Blanks – 361 - 380
(Exercise 19)

361. A boy tripped over a platform and then **b _ _ _ _ d** himself against the wall to break his fall.

362. Different plots would be pieced together to form a larger site for a civil **c _ _ _ _ _ _ _ e**.

363. Diplomatic relations officially resumed at the **s _ _ _ _ e** of midnight.

364. Flood is a **r _ _ _ _ _ _ _ g** problem here.

365. He had **s _ _ _ _ _ d** sharply to avoid a motorcyclist in his path.

366. I now feel that this was just **d _ _ _ _ _ _ d** to happen this way.

367. Inordinate delay in appointment of the commissioner is **h _ _ _ _ _ _ _ g** the fight against corruption.

368. Locals have stopped **v _ _ _ _ _ _ _ g** out in the dark.

369. Mobile tower **p _ _ _ d** serious health hazards.

370. Over the year, the number of deer **m_ _ _ _ _ _ _ _ d** and reached over 100, much above the parks' capacity.

371. People heard a loud **r _ _ _ _ _ g** noise.

372. Police officers were decorated with the President's medal for **d _ _ _ _ _ _ _ _ _ _ d** service.

373. President had rejected the bill owing to its **c _ _ _ _ _ _ _ _ _ _ _ _ l** provisions.

374. The road was cleared of debris and **e** _ _ _ _ _ _ _ _ _ _ **s**.

375. Stadium shall be **f** _ _ _ _ **d** and well-protected to prevent the entry of unauthorized persons.

376. The exact details will need to be **h** _ _ _ _ _ _ **d** out.

377. The sun was shining **w** _ _ _ _ **y**.

378. Their relationship **s** _ _ _ _ **d** over the last two months.

379. This is a shameful situation for a town which **t** _ _ _ _ _ **s** on tourism.

380. We are a **a** _ _ _ _ _ _ **d** and genuinely sorry that this happened.

ANSWERS

361. braced | 362. concourse | 363. stroke | 364. recurring | 365. swerved | 366. destined | 367. hindering | 368. venturing | 369. posed | 370. multiplied | 371. rumbling | 372. distinguished | 373. controversial | 374. encroachments | 375. fenced | 376. hammered | 377. warmly | 378. soured | 379. thrives | 380. appalled

Fill In the Blanks – 381 - 400
(Exercise 20)

381. A _ _ _ _ _ _ _ _ **y** there is no reason for not acting or relying upon the evidence of witnesses.

382. Both sides **i** _ _ _ **d** 20 agreements and three letters of intent.

383. Both sides showed no signs of **r** _ _ _ _ _ _ _ **g**.

384. Court **r** _ _ _ _ _ **d** the ban order passed by the local administration.

385. D _ _ _ _ _ e repeated attempts, the director of the hospital was unavailable for comments.

386. He f _ _ _ _ _ _ _ d a wrong affidavit in the court.

387. He had p _ _ _ _ d nets to trap a deer for poaching purposes.

388. He offered his condolences for those who died in the s _ _ _ _ _ _ e.

389. He won the battle with demons who h _ _ _ _ _ d his village.

390. Her good fortune v _ _ _ _ _ _ d.

391. I am only a _ _ _ _ _ _ _ _ _ d to speak on behalf of the party and its leaders and not their relatives.

392. Low-lying areas saw problems e _ _ _ _ _ _ _ _ _ d.

393. Supply of electricity could not be r _ _ _ _ _ _ d immediately in the villages.

394. The tremors, in a matter of few minutes, t _ _ _ _ _ _ _ _ d a big avalanche which swept away many climbers who were moving up.

395. There is no road l _ _ _ _ _ g right up to the village.

396. The train was taken off tracks last year following the broad gauge c _ _ _ _ _ _ _ _ n.

397. Two families were at d _ _ _ _ _ s drawn.

398. Vehicles broke down on many roads causing traffic s _ _ _ _ s.

399. We have no other option but to t _ _ _ _ _ _ _ e him since he took leave without informing the company.

400. We have not come across anything s _ _ _ _ _ _ _ _ s so far.

ANSWERS

381. apparently | **382.** inked | **383.** relenting | **384.** revoked | **385.** despite | **386.** furnished | **387.** placed | **388.** stampede | **389.** haunted |

390. vanished | **391.** authorized | **392.** exacerbated | **393.** restored | **394.** triggered | **395.** leading | **396.** conversion | **397.** daggers | **398.** snarls | **399.** terminate | **400.** suspicious

Fill In the Blanks – 401 - 420
(Exercise 21)

401. A prominent brand of refined oil was found to be selling a lesser quantity of oil than was **m** _ _ _ _ _ _ _ **d** as the net weight on the pack.

402. Cheating materials **i** _ _ _ _ _ _ **d** like bits of paper with notes written on them.

403. The city is growing at a **b** _ _ _ **k** pace.

404. Dates of voting would be **a** _ _ _ _ _ _ _ **d** later.

405. Employees were allegedly found making **f** _ _ _ _ _ _ _ _ _ **t** withdrawals of crop damage compensation.

406. Fighter jets **s** _ _ _ _ _ _ **d** through the sky.

407. He **c** _ _ _ _ _ **d** the stairs and reached the water tank.

408. He is mentally **d** _ _ _ _ _ _ _ _ _ **d**.

409. He says he never gave the issue much **c** _ _ _ _ _ _ _ _ _ _ _ **n**.

410. He showed the letters – with 'Government of India' **e** _ _ _ _ _ _ **d** on them.

411. High tension lines passing through **r** _ _ _ _ _ _ _ _ _ **l** areas and low hanging wires put their lives to risk every day.

412. In the area of culture, **p** _ _ _ _ _ _ _ _ **m** is the most demeaning blemish.

413. It was one of the most **d** _ _ _ _ _ _ **d** incidents during a fierce security crackdown.

414. Penalty for filing false affidavit **e** _ _ _ _ _ _ **d** a jail term of up to six months or fine or both.

415. Quake-induced landslide **w** _ _ _ **d** out roads.

416. Some areas received double the usual September rainfall in 48 hours, after **t** _ _ _ _ _ _ **l** storm.

417. The telescope is useful for research and study of **a** _ _ _ _ _ _ _ _ _ _ **l** events.

418. The game could have **s** _ _ _ **g** England's way.

419. Three sleeper coaches of the train **d** _ _ _ _ _ _ **d** in the incident.

420. The water tank was drained out and cleaned after **s** _ _ _ _ _ _ _ _ **g** bleaching powder.

ANSWERS

401. mentioned | 402. included | 403. brisk | 404. announced | 405. fraudulent | 406. screamed | 407. climbed | 408. disoriented | 409. consideration | 410. embossed | 411. residential | 412. plagiarism | 413. disputed | 414. entailed | 415. wiped | 416. tropical | 417. astronomical | 418. swung | 419. derailed | 420. sprinkling

Fill In the Blanks – 421 - 440
(Exercise 22)

421. 45% marks will be **e _ _ _ _ _ _ e** in seeking admission to these courses.

422. After **h _ _ _ _ _ g** discussions with others, we would decide our next step soon.

423. The sudden change of plan got him **m _ _ _ _ d.**

424. Authorities **s _ _ _ _ _ _ d** 20 doctors of their one day salary.

425. C **_ _ _ _ _ s** erupted between security forces and demonstrators.

426. The court lifted the ban **s _ _ _ _ _ d** by food regulators.

427. His office was **a _ _ _ z** with activity.

428. I **d _ _ _ _ _ _ _ _ e** any such irresponsible statement.

429. I have never experienced such a **f _ _ _ _ _ _ _ s** earthquake.

430. Incense smoke **w _ _ _ s** through the cold air.

431. Markets nosedived on global weakness caused by fears of **d _ _ _ _ _ _ _ _ _ n** of China currency Yuan.

432. Never before such an exercise has been taken in that **m _ _ _ _ _ e** scale.

433. Photographs showed **p _ _ _ _ s** of black smoke rising from the windows of one of the buildings.

434. Students were being asked to **t _ _ m** their hair for the past one week but they ignored it.

435. The match was well **c _ _ _ _ _ _ _ d.**

436. The roadshow **l _ _ _ _ d** for about 80 minutes.

437. There are 400 junior high schools **t _ _ _ _ _ _ _ _ t** the state.

438. They are suffering from various diseases with **d _ _ _ _ _ g** of garbage in the open.

439. We had no clue what had happened and were **s _ _ _ _ _ _ n** with fear.

440. We have no language to c _ _ _ _ _ n this.

ANSWERS

421. eligible | 422. holding | 423. miffed | 424. stripped | 425. clashes | 426. slapped | 427. abuzz | 428. disapprove | 429. ferocious | 430. wafts | 431. devaluation | 432. massive | 433. plumes | 434. trim | 435. contested | 436. lasted | 437. throughout | 438. dumping | 439. stricken | 440. condemn

Fill In the Blanks – 441 - 460
(Exercise 23)

441. A _ _ _ _ _ _ y was based on unverified information.

442. A person d _ _ _ _ n by greed for money can do anything.

443. E _ _ _ _ _ _ _ _ n of answer scripts was set to begin across the state from yesterday.

444. He t _ _ _ _ _ d over his shoelaces at a Megastore

445. He was a strong p _ _ _ _ _ _ _ t of the abolition of the death penalty.

446. He was seen counting the money and p _ _ _ _ _ _ _ g it in the video footage.

447. Incidents of a _ _ _ n and stone-pelting were reported from many parts of the city.

448. It took r _ _ _ _ _ y four hours to gain control over the situation.

449. Many farmers **s** _ _ _ _ _ _ _ **d** massive crop damage in the recent spell of unseasonal rain.

450. Many students **g** _ _ _ _ **d** for breath and suffered a terrible itch in the eyes.

451. Officers were trying to **c** _ _ _ _ _ _ **e** them not to take law in their hands.

452. Officials **c** _ _ _ _ _ _ _ **d** over $ 50,000 in fine.

453. People found **l** _ _ _ _ _ _ _ **g** will be penalized.

454. Plastic surgery made her look **u** _ _ _ _ _ _ **y**.

455. Police acted **s** _ _ _ _ _ **y** on a complaint.

456. Security forces were facing problems of **s** _ _ _ _ _ _ **e** of weapons and equipment.

457. Students will need to type in their registration number for **d** _ _ _ _ _ _ _ _ _ **g** the admit card.

458. The last date of submitting fees in many courses **l** _ _ _ _ **d** a few days ago.

459. The military said it was **r** _ _ _ _ _ _ _ _ _ **g** with aerial and ground strikes on their positions.

460. The roads are **f** _ _ _ _ _ _ **d** making it difficult for the students to commute.

ANSWERS

441. advisory | 442. driven | 443. evaluation | 444. tripped | 445. proponent | 446. pocketing | 447. arson | 448. roughly | 449. sustained | 450. gasped | 451. convince | 452. collected | 453. littering | 454.

ungainly | 455. swiftly | 456. shortage | 457. downloading | 458. lapsed | 459. responding | 460. furrowed

Fill In the Blanks – 461 - 480
(Exercise 24)

461. A series of earthquakes **j _ _ _ _ d** the residents here over the past two days.

462. College administration **f _ _ _ _ _ d** ignorance about police's midnight crackdown.

463. Complainants had to return empty-handed as senior official **c _ _ _ _ _ _ _ d** did not turn up.

464. Cops had to resort to light force to **d _ _ _ _ _ _ e** the crowd.

465. The government should **c _ _ _ _ y** a clear and positive message to investors.

466. He **a _ _ _ _ _ _ d** from the bus at the next step.

467. He had an **i _ _ _ _ _ g** that his end was near.

468. He has a stack of **h _ _ _ _ _ s** to overcome.

469. He is set to be elected **u _ _ _ _ _ _ _ d.**

470. Hearing his cries, local people **r _ _ _ _ d** to the spot and rescued her.

471. I am **d _ _ _ _ _ _ _ d** as false charges have been pressed against me.

472. Initial signs **s _ _ _ _ _ t** the fire started by accident.

473. Other families in the neighborhood had managed to **a _ _ _ _ _ e** the two feuding families.

474. R _ _ _ _ _ _ _ _ _ **t** will be done through the direct interview which may take a couple of years.

475. She **q** _ _ _ _ **d** up along with many others for a bus to her native village.

476. She was a bright student and rarely **m** _ _ _ _ **d** school.

477. She was **o** _ _ _ _ _ **d** to his criminal activities.

478. Some people were **e** _ _ _ _ _ _ _ _ _ _ _ **g** losses in order to receive compensation.

479. The mask **s** _ _ _ _ _ **d** off the face of him and his accomplice.

480. Those responsible for the attack will be **t** _ _ _ _ **d** and punished.

ANSWERS

461. jolted | **462.** feigned | **463.** concerned | **464.** disperse | **465.** convey | **466.** alighted | **467.** inkling | **468.** hurdles | **469.** unopposed | **470.** rushed | **471.** depressed | **472.** suggest | **473.** assuage | **474.** recruitment | **475.** queued | **476.** missed | **477.** opposed | **478.** exaggerating | **479.** slipped | **480.** traced

Fill In the Blanks – 481 - 500
(Exercise 25)

481. Drains remained **c** _ _ _ _ _ **d** with garbage and silt.

482. Fresh **m** _ _ _ **y** details emerged in the sensational murder case.

483. He had **d** _ _ _ _ **d** her with petrol and set him on fire.

484. He s _ _ _ _ _ _ d to bullet injuries during the course of treatment.

485. I felt slight t _ _ _ _ _ s around noon.

486. I was t _ _ _ _ _ _ d to see the superstars in front of me.

487. Party continued to e _ _ _ _ _ e a nonstop nationwide blockage.

488. President m _ _ _ _ _ d scathing attack on his rivals.

489. S _ _ _ _ _ g specific details will not be possible.

490. Child's rights activists l _ _ _ _ _ _ d an online campaign in protest against a cover story published in a bi-weekly magazine.

491. She agreed to rent out a shop at his a _ _ _ _ _ _ _ l house.

492. She has been c _ _ _ _ _ _ _ _ _ g with the probe.

493. European leaders needed to d _ _ _ _ e a common plan urgently to tackle the wave of migrants arriving in the bloc.

494. Some of the defaulter f _ _ _ _ _ _ d their proximity to senior bureaucrats.

495. Sometimes harsh decisions are r _ _ _ _ _ _ d to be taken.

496. The countdown was begun of her life as she was d _ _ _ _ _ _ _ d cancer.

497. Their car r _ _ _ _ d the central verge between two metro pillars.

498. There were tears in his eyes when he p _ _ _ _ d with his medals.

499. They h _ _ _ _ d trains to protest violence against migrants.

500. They saw buildings c _ _ _ _ _ e in front of their eyes.

ANSWERS

481. clogged | **482.** murky | **483.** doused | **484.** succumbed | **485.** tremors | **486.** thrilled | **487.** enforce | **488.** mounted | **489.** sharing | **490.** launched | **491.** ancestral | **492.** cooperating | **493.** devise | **494.**

flaunted | 495. required | 496. diagnosed | 497. rammed | 498. parted | 499. halted | 500. crumble

Fill In the Blanks – 501 - 520
(Exercise 26)

501. A modest weaver was **t _ _ _ _ _ g** hard on his handloom to finish a piece of the special stole.

502. A private bus skidded off the road following **c _ _ _ _ _ _ _ n** with a car.

503. The amount is yet to be **r _ _ _ _ _ _ _ d**.

504. An investigation is under process to **a _ _ _ _ _ _ _ n** the exact reason behind the attack.

505. Contaminated water had **s _ _ _ _ d** into the groundwater.

506. D _ _ _ _ _ _ _ _ s floods left fifty dead and dozens missing.

507. Do not **i _ _ _ _ _ e** your role models, do better than them.

508. Doctors could not save him as he had lost **c _ _ _ _ _ s** amounts of blood.

509. He admitted to the crime and also **r _ _ _ _ _ _ d** the involvement of two others.

510. He **d _ _ _ _ d** having any knowledge about it.

511. He voiced opposition to forestry policies **p _ _ _ _ _ _ d** by the govt.

512. Most rooms are yet to be **f _ _ _ _ d** with window frames.

513. Normalcy is **g _ _ _ _ _ _ _ y** returning to the violence-affected city.

514. She had been **s _ _ _ _ _ _ _ d** to cruelty and harassment by him.

515. The CCTV camera was i _ _ _ _ _ _ _ d on a wall.

516. The government should e _ _ _ _ e quick investigation in the case.

517. The residents also took out a c _ _ _ _ _ _ _ _ _ t vigil.

518. The two had confessed to have p _ _ _ _ _ d tigers.

519. There is a need to s _ _ _ _ _ _ _ _ n the security arrangements of the hospital.

520. We ensured that the workers' fears and tensions were a _ _ _ _ _ d.

ANSWERS

501. toiling | 502. collusion | 503. reimbursed | 504. ascertain | 505. seeped | 506. disastrous | 507. imitate | 508. copious | 509. revealed | 510. denied | 511. promoted | 512. fitted | 513. gradually | 514. subjected | 515. installed | 516. ensure | 517. candlelight | 518. poached | 519. strengthen | 520. allayed

Fill In the Blanks – 521 - 540
(Exercise 27)

521. A private school t _ _ _ _ _ _ d heads of 25 students to enforce discipline.

522. A squabble erupted over f _ _ _ _ _ g of voters' lists.

523. The accident left the front of the car c _ _ _ _ _ d.

524. Antlers of swamp deer were s _ _ _ _ d from them.

525. Both the sides decided not to p _ _ _ _ e the case further.

526. He went around the **c _ _ _ t** with folded hands.

527. The hearing has **r _ _ _ _ _ d** in a court after four years.

528. His family moved into a relief camp and received **m _ _ _ _ _ _ y** compensation.

529. I had no appetite and would not be able to **s _ _ _ _ _ w** anything.

530. Jails were **o _ _ _ _ _ _ d** far beyond capacity.

531. Scorpions are **n _ _ _ _ _ _ _ l** creatures.

532. Some trains witnessed route **d _ _ _ _ _ _ _ _ s**.

533. The bank held interest rates **s _ _ _ _ y**.

534. The house owner had illegally **h _ _ _ _ d** onto an overhead electricity line through a cable running from his house.

535. The police were **t _ _ _ _ d** off that the men in the car were wanted criminals.

536. They also **r _ _ _ _ d** slogans against the state government.

537. They **e _ _ _ _ _ _ _ d** restraint while speaking.

538. Untreated biomedical waste can **i _ _ _ _ e** spread of communicable diseases.

539. Whosoever has a problem is free to **a _ _ _ _ _ _ _ h** the court.

540. Winter chill **s _ _ _ _ _ _ d**.

ANSWERS

521. tonsured | 522. fudging | 523. crushed | 524. seized | 525. pursue | 526. casket | 527. resumed | 528. monetary | 529. swallow | 530. occupied | 531. nocturnal | 532. diversions | 533. steady | 534. hooked | 535. tipped | 536. raised | 537. exercised | 538. induce | 539. approach | 540. subsided

Fill In the Blanks – 541 - 560

(Exercise 28)

541. A broad agreement has been **a _ _ _ _ d** at between the parties on all issues.

542. A **t _ _ _ _ e** broke out between him and other youths over some issue at the function.

543. All was not well with the way cases relating to grant of bail were being **h _ _ _ _ _ d**.

544. Any delay in the treatment could have proved **f _ _ _ l**.

545. Broad **c _ _ _ _ _ _ _ s** has emerged for a symbol.

546. He narrated the **o _ _ _ _ l** to his colleagues who took her to the police.

547. He was at a **d _ _ _ _ _ _ t** position.

548. He was unable to **r _ _ _ _ t** superstition.

549. Many buildings had become dangerous to **i _ _ _ _ _ t** after the earthquake.

550. People fled out of their homes and offices in **p _ _ _ c**.

551. They will play a crucial role in **s _ _ _ _ _ g** the matter.

552. President took a **d _ _ _ _ _ _ d** meeting on the proposed law.

553. She made a very **e _ _ _ _ _ _ t** but hollow speech.

554. Some leaders have little **r _ _ _ _ d** for human values.

555. The heat seems to have made the city come to a **s _ _ _ _ _ _ _ _ l**.

556. There is willful **c _ _ _ _ _ _ _ _ _ t** of identity on her part.

557. There were no reports of any **s** _ _ _ _ _ **e** between the two rival groups.

558. This building is old and can turn to **r** _ _ _ _ **e** anytime.

559. Three feet of snow **p** _ _ _ **d** up.

560. Tons of debris **c** _ _ _ _ **d** drains along the road.

ANSWERS

541. arrived | 542. tussle | 543. handled | 544. fatal | 545. consensus | 546. ordeal | 547. dominant | 548. resist | 549. inhabit | 550. panic | 551. sorting | 552. detailed | 553. eloquent | 554. regard | 555. standstill | 556. concealment | 557. scuffle | 558. rubble | 559. piled | 560. choked

Fill In the Blanks – 561 - 580
(Exercise 29)

561. A high voltage transfer **e** _ _ _ _ _ _ **d** suddenly.

562. A motorist **c** _ _ _ _ _ _ **d** with a cow and fell into a garbage dump.

563. A portion of the vehicle's floor **c** _ _ _ **d** in and the boy fell through.

564. Bird census method was **f** _ _ _ _ **d**.

565. A chopper **c** _ _ _ _ _ **d** due to a technical fault while landing.

566. The city reported numerous **i** _ _ _ _ _ _ _ _ **s** of monkey bites every day.

567. Court **s** _ _ _ _ **t** the status report on the investigation into the case.

568. Diesel **f** _ _ _ **s** cause damages to the lungs.

569. Government departments are busy pushing blame on each other to tackle the **m _ _ _ _ e**.

570. He was lucky to survive the series of explosions that **r _ _ _ _ d** his dormitory.

571. His message **e _ _ _ _ _ _ d** 2,000 comments.

572. I have been **c _ _ _ _ _ _ d** within four walls of my house.

573. Police **c_ _ _ _ _ _ _ d** pat-down searches.

574. The principal warned against **d _ _ _ _ _ g** premature conclusion.

575. Profiteering has become **r _ _ _ _ _ t**.

576. Riot police were a **a _ _ _ _ _ _ _ _ g** to block protestors from entering the building.

577. S _ _ _ _ _ l passed through the villages of the state.

578. The park **s _ _ _ _ _ _ _ s** over 30 acres.

579. We are hopeful that everyone will **a _ _ _ _ e** to instructions.

580. We **d _ _ _ _ _ _ _ _ _ _ d** information about these through various modes of communication.

ANSWERS

561. exploded | 562. collided | 563. caved | 564. flawed | 565. crashed | 566. instances | 567. sought | 568. fumes | 569. menace | 570. rocked | 571. elicited | 572. confined | 573. conducted | 574. drawing | 575. rampant | 576. attempting | 577. several | 578. stretches | 579. adhere | 580. disseminated

Fill In the Blanks – 581 - 600
(Exercise 30)

581. A proposal is being **c** _ _ _ _ _ _ _ _ **d** to build new jails in four districts.

582. All authorities have utterly failed to **c** _ _ _ _ **y** with the directions of the Tribunal.

583. Bodies were **e** _ _ _ _ _ _ _ **d** from the ruins.

584. Bomb disposal squad is **e** _ _ _ _ _ _ _ **g** the scene.

585. Cops allegedly tortured him to **c** _ _ _ _ _ **s** to the crime.

586. He had **e** _ _ _ _ _ **d** a team of painters for whitewashing.

587. His campaign came to a **n** _ _ _ _ **t**.

588. I lost a lot of **r** _ _ _ _ _ **t** for him after all this.

589. Judge **e** _ _ _ _ _ _ _ _ **d** him of all the charges.

590. Our revenue **d** _ _ _ _ **d** considerably.

591. People tend to take more food on their plates than they could **c** _ _ _ _ _ **e**.

592. Police will **d** _ _ _ _ _ _ **e** the motive behind the complaint.

593. Scorching summers or freezing cold, nothing **d** _ _ _ _ **s** him.

594. She refused to marry him **c** _ _ _ _ **g** the difference in their faiths.

595. Students **f** _ _ _ _ _ **d** hostel rules on a regular basis and got punished.

596. The yield this year **s** _ _ _ _ **s** at about 50 tonnes.

597. These institutions have no record of **d** _ _ _ _ _ _ **l** of grievances.

598. They bid tearful **a** _ _ _ **u** to him.

599. Association members **c** _ _ _ _ _ _ _ _ **d** police action on media personnel.

600. They had been awaiting the government's **a** _ _ _ _ _ _ **l**.

ANSWERS

581. considered | 582. comply | 583. extracted | 584. examining | 585. confess | 586. engaged | 587. naught | 588. respect | 589. exonerated | 590. dipped | 591. consume | 592. disclose | 593. deters | 594. citing | 595. flouted | 596. stands | 597. disposal | 598. adieu | 599. condemned | 600. approval

Fill In the Blanks – 601 - 620
(Exercise 31)

601. A major fire **s** _ _ _ _ _ **d** communication services in the area.

602. Around 1 million answer scripts **a**_ _ _ _ _ **d** evaluation.

603. Convert the global **t** _ _ _ _ _ **l** into an opportunity.

604. Fear of dengue has once again **g** _ _ _ _ _ **d** the city.

605. He had no information on who would be **r** _ _ _ _ _ _ _ **g** the doctors who had been transferred or when.

606. He made most of his **o**_ _ _ _ _ _ _ _ _ **y**.

607. He **r** _ _ _ _ _ _ **d** that driving was a stable profession with scope for a good income.

608. He was **e** _ _ _ _ _ _ _ _ **g** loss due to hail storm and heavy rainfall in the region.

609. His mortal remains were **c _ _ _ _ _ _ _ d** to flames with full Army honors.

610. Homes were found to lack basic **a _ _ _ _ _ _ _ s** and were sealed by the district administration.

611. I admire him for his service to the poor and **d _ _ _ _ _ _ _ e**.

612. If he was booked, he could be **i _ _ _ _ _ _ _ _ d** for life.

613. It is a matter of grave concern that people are sending false and **f _ _ _ _ _ _ _ s** complaints.

614. Phone services were **c _ _ _ _ _ _ _ d**.

615. Some lenders have expected the bad loan situation to **w _ _ _ _ n** in coming years.

616. The storm **k _ _ _ _ _ d** out power to nearly 25,000 customers in the city.

617. They should adopt **p _ _ _ _ _ _ _ _ _ _ _ y** measures and not let their children play alone in open.

618. They will **s _ _ _ m** the streets singing patriotic songs.

619. The deficit rainfall is set to pull down the crop **y _ _ _ d** this year.

620. Cops acted **p _ _ _ _ _ _ y** and sealed all the city crossings, highways and check-posts.

ANSWERS

601. severed | 602. awaited | 603. turmoil | 604. gripped | 605. replacing | 606. opportunity | 607. realized | 608. estimating | 609. consigned | 610. amenities | 611. destitute | 612. imprisoned | 613. frivolous | 614. curtailed | 615. worsen | 616. knocked | 617. precautionary | 618. swarm | 619. yield | 620. promptly

Fill In the Blanks – 621 - 640
(Exercise 32)

621. A **g** _ _ _ _ _ **y** road accident could have occurred when the driver dozed off at the wheels.

622. An overcrowded mechanized boat carrying nearly 200 people **c** _ _ _ _ _ _ **d** in the river.

623. Security of judges have been **b** _ _ _ _ **d** up.

624. C _ _ _ _ _ _ _ _ **n** is not something that should be reserved only for festival periods.

625. Court also **s** _ _ _ _ _ **d** on the convicts a hefty sum of one million dollars as fine.

626. Dense fog **d** _ _ _ _ _ _ **s** rail traffic in winter.

627. She **I** _ _ _ _ _ **d** incense sticks.

628. G _ _ _ _ _ _ _ _ _ _ _ **n** is a boon for students as it has given them a chance to study in any country they want.

629. He is a player with **a** _ _ _ _ _ _ **t** talent, a delight to watch when in full flow.

630. He was in the midst of a hair transplant **p** _ _ _ _ _ _ _ **e** in a clinic when the power went off.

631. It is a shameful act; no one involved will be **s** _ _ _ _ **d**.

632. Just 25 minutes of **b** _ _ _ **k** walking a day can add up to seven years to your life.

633. Many bureaucrats say **a _ _ _ _ t** replacement of top officials creates uncertainty.

634. Massive security has been **d _ _ _ _ _ _ d** in the village following tension in the area.

635. People found to be **i _ _ _ _ _ _ _ g** in illegal activities will have to pay a huge penalty.

636. Photo stories have the tendency to **e _ _ _ e** an emotion.

637. Police were trying to **c _ _ _ _ _ _ _ _ _ e** the information given by the militants.

638. There have been instances when he didn't **a _ _ _ _ e** to the spirit of the game.

639. This video was apparently **c _ _ _ _ _ _ _ d** by a German correspondent.

640. Trees are being lost at an **a _ _ _ _ _ _ g** rate because of human activities.

ANSWERS

621. ghastly | **622. capsized** | **623. beefed** | **624. compassion** | **625. slapped** | **626. disrupts** | **627. lighted** | **628. globalization** | **629. abundant** | **630. procedure** | **631. spared** | **632. brisk** | **633. abrupt** | **634. deployed** | **635. indulging** | **636. evoke** | **637. corroborate** | **638. adhere** | **639. captured** | **640. alarming**

Fill In the Blanks – 641 - 660
(Exercise 33)

641. A man with an air gun was **d _ _ _ _ _ _ d** when he tried to enter President's rally venue.

642. All of us love to get a glimpse of the off-duty look of **c _ _ _ _ _ _ _ _ _ s**, especially their family moments.

643. Around 80 people are feared to be trapped inside a boat which **c _ _ _ _ _ _ d** yesterday.

644. Auditor raised a number of objections related to **i _ _ _ _ _ _ d** travel expenses by experts hired by the Examination Board.

645. Chief Minister called upon the police personnel to **c _ _ _ _ _ t** crime investigations "efficiently and effectively."

646. A **_ _ _ _ _ _ _ _ _ _ _ _ n** in the district has collapsed and people wanted a change in government.

647. The court directed the government to **e _ _ _ _ _ _ _ h** dispensaries in jails.

648. Exposure to smoke and dust can **a _ _ _ _ _ _ _ e** asthma attacks.

649. He found household items lying **s _ _ _ _ _ _ _ d** all over the place.

650. He has a history of making **c _ _ _ _ _ _ _ _ _ _ _ l** remarks about lawyers.

651. Court verdict drew mixed responses from the legal **f _ _ _ _ _ _ _ _ y** and political parties.

652. He made an **o _ _ _ _ _ _ g** of 5 million dollars at the eye hospital.

653. It was one of the most **e _ _ _ _ _ _ g** mysteries that have baffled three generations of truth-seekers.

654. The oil minister was right in describing the new policy cleared by the Cabinet as a **p _ _ _ _ _ _ m** shift.

655. Police **t _ _ _ d** the car provider who allegedly gave the vehicle used in the crime.

656. Police wanted to beat a **c _ _ _ _ _ _ _ _ n** out of him!

657. Sun is the **v _ _ _ l** source of energy for all beings.

658. Their bilateral ties were **d _ _ _ _ _ _ _ _ _ _ _ g** faster than anyone expected.

659. While two **m _ _ _ _ _ d** to escape, the other two were caught.

660. Women like men deserve opportunities to fulfill their **p _ _ _ _ _ _ _ l,** no matter where they live,"

ANSWERS

641. detained | 642. celebrities | 643. capsized | 644. inflated | 645. conduct | 646. administration | 647. establish | 648. aggravate | 649. scattered | 650. controversial | 651. fraternity | 652. offering | 653. enduring | 654. paradigm | 655. traced | 656. confession | 657. vital | 658. deteriorating | 659. managed | 660. potential

Fill In the Blanks – 661 - 680
(Exercise 34)

661. He was named as one of the winners of the **p _ _ _ _ _ _ _ _ _ s** award.

662. An award is a r _ _ _ _ _ _ _ _ n of intellectual, literary, creative or academic merits.

663. Assembly was adjourned within ten minutes of c _ _ _ _ _ _ _ g following an uproar by Opposition members.

664. Authorities have been asked to rope in locals for development i _ _ _ _ _ _ _ _ e.

665. Classrooms were of smaller size than required under p _ _ _ _ _ _ _ _ g norms.

666. Drought relief compensation is still to be d _ _ _ _ _ _ _ d.

667. A _ _ _ _ _ _ e provisions have not been made available to them.

668. Evaluating big data can be confusing and potentially o _ _ _ _ _ _ _ _ _ _ g for businesses.

669. Fake identification documents were also recovered from his p _ _ _ _ _ _ _ _ n.

670. He was awarded for exposing illegal mining and land g _ _ _ _ _ _ g activities.

671. The financial crisis was one of the reasons behind their f _ _ _ _ _ _ t quarrels.

672. He was using fake registration plates on the vehicles to e _ _ _ _ e from police.

673. I am f _ _ _ _ _ _ g out my legal rights to take the right steps ahead in this matter.

674. No FIR has been filed so far against them for making i _ _ _ _ _ _ _ _ _ _ y comments.

675. Our plan is being c _ _ _ _ _ d out.

676. Security forces had l _ _ _ _ _ _ d a massive operation, following information about the presence of a group of militants in the area.

677. She does not wish to have her real name **r** _ _ _ _ _ _ **d**.

678. The department was **g** _ _ _ _ _ _ _ **g** with an acute shortage of staff.

679. The excitement was **p** _ _ _ _ _ _ **e** on the faces of many in the crowd.

680. Whatever they have finally **o** _ _ _ _ _ **d** is not acceptable to us.

ANSWERS

661. prestigious | 662. recognition | 663. convening | 664. initiative |
665. prevailing | 666. disbursed | 667. adequate | 668. overwhelming |
669. possession | 670. grabbing | 671. frequent | 672. escape | 673.
figuring | 674. inflammatory | 675. chalked | 676. launched | 677.
revealed | 678. grappling | 679. palpable | 680. offered

Fill In the Blanks – 681 - 700
(Exercise 35)

681. Controversy has once again brought **f** _ _ _ _ _ _ _ _ _ _ **m** within the party.

682. Each time we are given **a** _ _ _ _ _ _ _ _ _ **s** and asked to end our strike.

683. If you talk again you will be **e** _ _ _ _ _ _ **d** out of the examination hall.

684. Exercise is the **e** _ _ _ _ **r** for good bones and hence good health.

685. F _ _ _ _ _ **e** and soreness at the initial stages of the workout are normal.

686. Foreign countries **w** _ _ _ _ _ **d** up search and rescue operations.

687. General Coach was packed beyond **c** _ _ _ _ _ _ _ **y**.

688. Good wishes and congratulations **p _ _ _ _ d** in for him from old teammates.

689. He was seen **w _ _ _ _ _ _ g** guests with folded hands.

690. Security was **s _ _ _ _ _ d** up across the nation.

691. No **o _ _ _ _ _ _ e** could dampen enthusiastic spirits of contestants.

692. People often **o _ _ _ _ _ _ k** their health for money and consider work to be more important.

693. Potato is an **i _ _ _ _ _ _ l** part of every kitchen.

694. The day began with much **s _ _ _ _ _ _ _ _ _ n** among the participants as well as the crowd present.

695. The entire crop was damaged by **e _ _ _ _ _ _ _ e** and unseasonal rainfall.

696. They were **p _ _ _ _ _ _ d** a lot and given very little.

697. To be successful, one must know the art of time **m _ _ _ _ _ _ _ _ t.**

698. Without hard work, you cannot reach the heights of **g _ _ _ y.**

699. Work is on to repair the **b _ _ _ _ n** boundary walls, gates and leveling the ground.

700. Work of a constable is quite **t _ _ _ _ _ s** and hazardous.

ANSWERS

681. factionalism | 682. assurances | 683. escorted | 684. elixir | 685. fatigue | 686. wrapped | 687. capacity | 688. poured | 689. welcoming | 690. stepped | 691. obstacle | 692. overlook | 693. integral | 694. speculation | 695. excessive | 696. promised | 697. management | 698. glory | 699. broken | 700. tedious

Fill In the Blanks – 701 - 710

(Exercise 36)

LONG SENTENCES

701. A "life-threatening" **b _ _ _ _ _ _ d** barreled into the US northeast, affecting up to 20% of Americans as it kept workers and students housebound, **h _ _ _ _ d** thousands of fights and prompted officials to ban cars from roads and **s _ _ _ _ _ _ n** public transport.

702. A **m _ _ _ _ _ _ y** of locals decided not to clear their **p _ _ _ _ _ g** bills, forcing the power officials to **r _ _ _ _ _ _ t** power supply to the areas.

703. District authorities and forest department officials have been **q _ _ _ _ _ _ _ g** over jurisdictions **i _ _ _ _ s** with the forest department refusing to take action against the stray dogs saying the animals did not come under their **p _ _ _ _ _ w**.

704. No one would have ever imagined that people may **a _ _ _ _ _ e** a postgraduate degree first, **f _ _ _ _ _ _ d** by an undergraduate degree, and thereafter complete the higher secondary course, eventually to go to a **k _ _ _ _ _ _ _ _ _ _ n**.

705. This project is **u _ _ _ _ e** in the sense that no land has been acquired, no trees **u _ _ _ _ _ _ d**, no forests destroyed and the entire plant has been built on ash **d _ _ _ s**.

706. A fresh **s _ _ _ l** of snowfall was experienced in the upper reaches of the state while light to **m _ _ _ _ _ _ e** rainfall was **w _ _ _ _ _ _ _ d** in other parts.

707. A **s _ _ _ _ _ _ g** truck reportedly **k _ _ _ _ _ d** over an electric pole, breaking wires and leading to a **b _ _ _ _ _ _ t** on Saturday night.

708. President mounted a **b _ _ _ _ _ _ _ _ g** attack on the opposition parties accusing them of **s _ _ _ _ _ _ _ g** misgivings and confusion about the bill while claiming its government has ended the policy **p _ _ _ _ _ _ _ s** and the "reign of scams" of the past.

709. To a question on the **c _ _ _ _ _ _ _ _ _ s** absence of the minister and some other prominent peoples' representatives at the program, he said it could have been because of their **p _ _ _ _ _ _ _ _ _ _ _ n** with some other **p _ _ _ _ _ _ g** engagements.

710. The power department's **a _ _ _ _ _ _ _ t** drive, which started on Jan 10 seems to have **g _ _ _ _ _ _ d** success with **a _ _ _ _ _ s** to the tune of dollar 5 million being collected in the past month and a half.

ANSWERS

701. blizzard, halted, shutdown | 702. majority, pending, restrict | 703. quibbling, issues, purview | 704. acquire, followed, kindergarten | 705. unique, uprooted, dykes | 706. spell, moderate, witnessed | 707. speeding, knocked, blackout | 708. blistering, spreading, paralysis | 709. conspicuous, preoccupation, pressing | 710. antitheft, garnered, arrears

Fill In the Blanks – 711 - 720
(Exercise 37)

LONG SENTENCES

711. City s _ _ _ _ _ _ _ _ g at 45 degrees Celsius, several localities were for hours p _ _ _ _ _ d into darkness due to e _ _ _ _ _ c power supply.

712. Complaints of t _ _ _ y aid distribution piled up despite a g _ _ t of relief material c _ _ _ _ _ _ g the airport and relief hubs.

713. Considering the seriousness and s _ _ _ _ _ _ _ _ _ y of the case and also the fact the place of i _ _ _ _ _ _ t is very close to the border area, the government has decided to e _ _ _ _ _ t investigation of the case to FBI.

714. Earthquake o _ _ _ _ _ _ _ _ d in Nepal shook large parts of northern and eastern India, d _ _ _ _ _ _ g houses and buildings and s _ _ _ _ _ _ g panic among the people.

715. The department **i** _ _ _ _ _ **s** to start a massive awareness campaign among passengers asking them to **r** _ _ _ _ _ **n** from carrying **i** _ _ _ _ _ _ _ _ _ **e** substance during a bus journey.

716. Their panic was **t** _ _ _ _ _ _ _ _ **d** by the fact that around 50 school buildings are in a **d** _ _ _ _ _ _ _ _ _ _ **d** condition and the recent tremors could have led to **u** _ _ _ _ _ _ **d** incident.

717. Online procedure spared us from the **o** _ _ _ _ **l** of standing in a long queue in **s** _ _ _ _ _ _ _ _ **g** heat first to collect and thereafter **d** _ _ _ _ _ **t** the admission form at different countries set up by university authorities.

718. Power officials said the heavy rains **c** _ _ _ _ _ **d** with lightning and thunderbolts **u** _ _ _ _ _ _ **d** several trees which fell on power lines and **s** _ _ _ _ _ **d** them, besides damaging electricity poles in several areas of the city.

719. President won **m** _ _ _ _ _ **e** by a margin that would make words like 'landslide' and 'overwhelming' sound **l** _ _ _ _ _ _ **s** and **f** _ _ _ _ **e**.

720. State governments **i** _ _ _ _ **d** a public warning directing people to drink a lot of fluids and **a** _ _ _ _ _ _ **h** the nearest hospital in case of any symptoms of **s** _ _ _ _ _ _ _ **e**.

ANSWERS

711. sweltering, plunged, erratic | 712. tardy, glut, clogging | 713. sensitivity, incident, entrust | 714. originated, damaging, sparking | 715. intends, refrain, inflammable | 716. triggered, dilapidated, untoward | 717. ordeal, scorching, deposit | 718. coupled, uprooted, snapped | 719. mandate, listless, feeble | 720. issued, approach, sunstroke

Fill In the Blanks – 721 - 730
(Exercise 38)

LONG SENTENCES

721. He c _ _ _ _ d atop an overhead water tank to protest against the district administration's order to v _ _ _ _ e the house a _ _ _ _ _ _ d to him.

722. R _ _ _ _ _ d by the tragedy, the government was m _ _ _ _ _ g to bring in a harsher law to deal with b _ _ _ _ _ _ _ _ g.

723. The p _ _ _ _ _ _ _ _ y of generals, admirals and air marshals to increasingly f _ _ _ _ t their rank and status at all times, whether playing golf or driving personal cars, has the three Service headquarters worried due to growing social o _ _ _ _ _ _ _ m

724. He **i** _ _ _ _ _ _ _ **d** with officials and also **i** _ _ _ _ _ _ **d** the quality of road being **c** _ _ _ _ _ _ _ _ **d** by State Highway Authority.

725. Home guards posted on duty **p** _ _ _ _ **d** upon him, **s** _ _ _ _ _ _ **d** the matches and **o** _ _ _ _ _ _ _ _ **d** him.

726. Panicked city residents **r** _ _ _ **d** out of their houses and workplaces and **a** _ _ _ _ _ _ _ **d** in open places.

727. A surprise inspection by the district magistrate **r** _ _ _ _ _ _ **d** that the science center was in a **d** _ _ _ _ _ _ _ _ **e** state.

728. UFO **e** _ _ _ _ _ **d** bright light that formed a circle and also **r** _ _ _ _ _ **d** a range of colors.

729. Spying dragnet has **e** _ _ _ _ _ _ _ _ **d** a deep distrust at the highest **e** _ _ _ _ _ _ **s** of international leadership.

730. He **c** _ _ _ _ _ _ _ **d** that political parties in power have significant control over **l** _ _ _ _ _ _ _ _ _ _ **s** and executive and the people have the right to know about their **f** _ _ _ _ _ _ _ _ _ **g** in a democratic country.

ANSWERS

721. climbed, vacate, allotted | 722. rattled, mulling, bootlegging | 723. propensity, flaunt, opprobrium | 724. interacted, inspected, constructed | 725. pounced, snatched, overpowered | 726. rushed,

assembled | 727. revealed, deplorable | 728. emitted, radiated | 729. engendered, echelons | 730. contended, legislatures, functioning

Fill In the Blanks – 731 - 740
(Exercise 39)

LONG SENTENCES

731. The health department has put up posters and is distributing **p _ _ _ _ _ _ _ s** among city residents to stress the importance of cleanliness and **h _ _ _ _ _ e** in **p _ _ _ _ _ _ _ _ g** dengue fever.

732. l _ _ _ _ _ _ _ t rains **l _ _ _ _ d** large parts of the state causing floods and **l _ _ _ _ _ _ _ _ s** leaving more than 100 people dead so far.

733. He **p _ _ _ _ d** a wreath, **o _ _ _ _ _ d** his final salute and **s _ _ _ d** in silence in front of her body.

734. Highly motivated and **d _ _ _ _ _ _ _ d** followers have made it their mission to live and die for him and **e _ _ _ _ _ _ _ e** anyone they see as an **i _ _ _ _ _ _ _ _ t** to their leader.

735. In a **b _ _ _ _ _ e** incident, a vulture **r _ _ _ _ d** into the windscreen of the train engine, breaking through the glass and **l _ _ _ _ _ g** inside.

736. An underground cable was hit by a technical **s _ _ g** that left **a _ _ _ _ _ _ g** areas **s _ _ _ _ d** of power supply for over 20 hours.

737. Court agreed to examine whether the sentences were **d _ _ _ _ _ _ _ _ _ _ _ e** to the crime as the convicts **p _ _ _ _ d** for **l _ _ _ _ _ y**.

738. Roads users have had a long-standing **g _ _ _ _ e** that they were **f _ _ _ _ _ d** by concessionaires who charged a hefty toll on stretches of **d _ _ _ _ _ _ _ _ d** national highways.

739. As soon as the **p _ _ _ _ _ _ _ _ _ s** commenced, his counsel moved the plea, saying it should be heard before arguments on **f _ _ _ _ _ g** of charges as the matter **i _ _ _ _ _ s** legal issues.

740. **C _ _ _ _ _ _ g** down on schools running without **a _ _ _ _ _ _ _ _ _ n** papers, the district education officers **s _ _ _ _ d** closure notices to the two schools.

ANSWERS

731. pamphlets, hygiene, preventing | 732. incessant, lashed, landslides | 733. placed, offered, stood | 734. dedicated, eliminate, impediment | 735. bizarre, rammed, landing | 736. snag, adjoining, starved | 737. disproportionate, pleaded, leniency | 738. grouse, fleeced, dilapidated | 739. proceedings, framing, involves | 740. cracking, affiliation, served

Fill In the Blanks – 741 - 750
(Exercise 40)

LONG SENTENCES

741. V _ _ _ _ _ **g** disappointment over being dropped as a minister, he **l** _ _ _ _ **d** out at the party leadership for not having the **c** _ _ _ _ _ _ **y** to inform him about the decision first.

742. European countries **g** _ _ _ _ _ _ **d** with record numbers of **d** _ _ _ _ _ _ _ **e** refugees and migrants **c** _ _ _ _ _ _ _ **g** to enter Europe.

743. Labor law **r** _ _ _ _ _ **s** are crucial and important to create **c** _ _ _ _ _ _ _ **e** environment for investments and employment **g** _ _ _ _ _ _ _ _ **n** in the country.

744. The rains first **b** _ _ _ _ _ **d** the wheat grain, which burst out of the **k** _ _ _ _ **l** and got exposed to the sun, and **s** _ _ _ _ _ _ _ **d**.

745. Three **m** _ _ _ _ **d** men entered office premises after **d** _ _ _ _ _ _ **g** a hole in the wall and **d** _ _ _ _ _ _ **d** with computers.

746. Dengue is caused by mosquitoes that **b** _ _ _ **d** in containers and **s** _ _ _ _ _ _ **t** water around the **d** _ _ _ _ _ _ _ **s**.

747. His facial muscles **t _ _ _ _ _ _ d**, lips **q _ _ _ _ _ _ d** and eyes turned misty as he strived to utter something, **s _ _ _ _ _ _ _ d** and then gave up.

748. This move is aimed at convincing the government to **a _ _ _ _ _ _ e** its **r _ _ _ _ _ _ _ t** and **r _ _ _ _ _ _ _ _ e** prohibition policy.

749. Retail counters do not strictly follow **m _ _ _ _ _ _ _ y** guidelines for selling SIM cards, leaving enough scope for misuse of SIM cards, **p _ _ _ _ _ _ d** through **f _ _ _ _ d** identifies in committing crimes.

750. Driver **p _ _ _ _ _ _ _ _ _ y** lost control of his speeding vehicle and hit a tree, before **r _ _ _ _ _ g** into and breaking a **p _ _ _ _ _ t**.

ANSWERS

741. voicing, lashed, courtesy | 742. grappled, desperate, clamoring | 743. reforms, conducive, generation | 744. bloated, kernel, shriveled | 745. masked, drilling, decamped | 746. breed, stagnant, dwellings | 747. twitched, quivered, stuttered | 748. abdicate, redundant, regressive | 749. mandatory, procured, forged | 750. purportedly, ramming, parapet

****

About the Author

Manik Joshi was born on January 26, 1979, at Ranikhet, a picturesque town in the Kumaon region of the Indian state of Uttarakhand. He is a permanent resident of the Sheeshmahal area of Kathgodam located in the city of Haldwani in the Kumaon region of Uttarakhand in India. He completed his schooling in four different schools. He is a science graduate in the ZBC – zoology, botany, and chemistry – subjects. He is also an MBA with a specialization in marketing. Additionally, he holds diplomas in "computer applications", "multimedia and web-designing", and "computer hardware and networking". During his schooldays, he wanted to enter the field of medical science; however, after graduation, he shifted his focus to the field of management. After obtaining his MBA, he enrolled in a computer education center; he became so fascinated with working on the computer that he decided to develop his career in this field. Over the following years, he worked at some computer-related full-time jobs. Following that, he became interested in Internet Marketing, particularly in domaining (business of buying and selling domain names), web design (creating websites), and various other online jobs. However, later he shifted his focus solely to self-publishing. Manik is a nature-lover. He has always been fascinated by overcast skies. He is passionate about traveling and enjoys solo travel most of the time rather than traveling in groups. He is actually quite a loner who prefers to do his own thing. He likes to listen to music, particularly when he is working on the computer. Reading and writing are definitely his favorite pastimes, but he has no interest in sports. Manik has always dreamed of a prosperous life and prefers to live a life of luxury. He has a keen interest in politics because he believes it is politics that decides everything else. He feels a sense of gratification sharing his experiences and knowledge with the outside world. However, he is an introvert by nature and thus gives prominence to only a few people in his personal life. He is not a spiritual man, yet he actively seeks knowledge about the metaphysical world; he is particularly interested in learning about life beyond death. In addition to writing academic/informational text and fictional content, he also maintains a personal diary. He has always had a desire to stand out from the crowd. He does not believe in treading the beaten path and avoids copying someone else's path to success. Two things he always refrains from are smoking and drinking; he is a teetotaler and very health-conscious. He usually wakes up before the sun rises. He starts his morning with meditation and exercise. Fitness is an integral and indispensable part of his life. He gets energized by solving complex problems. He loves himself the way he is and he loves the way he looks. He doesn't believe in following fashion trends. He dresses according to what suits him & what he is comfortable in. He believes in taking calculated risks. His philosophy is to expect the best but prepare for the worst. According to him, you can't succeed if you are unwilling to fail. For Manik, life is about learning from mistakes and figuring out how to move forward.

Amazon Author Page of Manik Joshi:
https://www.amazon.com/author/manikjoshi
Email: manik85joshi@gmail.com

BIBLIOGRAPHY

(A). SERIES TITLE: "ENGLISH DAILY USE" *[40 BOOKS]*

01. How to Start a Sentence
02. English Interrogative Sentences
03. English Imperative Sentences
04. Negative Forms In English
05. Learn English Exclamations
06. English Causative Sentences
07. English Conditional Sentences
08. Creating Long Sentences In English
09. How to Use Numbers In Conversation
10. Making Comparisons In English
11. Examples of English Correlatives
12. Interchange of Active and Passive Voice
13. Repetition of Words
14. Remarks In the English Language
15. Using Tenses In English
16. English Grammar- Am, Is, Are, Was, Were
17. English Grammar- Do, Does, Did
18. English Grammar- Have, Has, Had
19. English Grammar- Be and Have
20. English Modal Auxiliary Verbs
21. Direct and Indirect Speech
22. Get- Popular English Verb
23. Ending Sentences with Prepositions
24. Popular Sentences In English
25. Common English Sentences
26. Daily Use English Sentences
27. Speak English Sentences Every Day
28. Popular English Idioms and Phrases
29. Common English Phrases
30. Daily English- Important Notes
31. Collocations In the English Language
32. Words That Act as Multiple Parts of Speech (Part 1)
33. Words That Act as Multiple Parts of Speech (Part 2)
34. Nouns In the English Language
35. Regular and Irregular Verbs
36. Transitive and Intransitive Verbs

37. 10,000 Useful Adjectives In English
38. 4,000 Useful Adverbs In English
39. 20 Categories of Transitional Expressions
40. How to End a Sentence

****

(B). SERIES TITLE: "ENGLISH WORD POWER" *[30 BOOKS]*

01. Dictionary of English Synonyms
02. Dictionary of English Antonyms
03. Homonyms, Homophones and Homographs
04. Dictionary of English Capitonyms
05. Dictionary of Prefixes and Suffixes
06. Dictionary of Combining Forms
07. Dictionary of Literary Words
08. Dictionary of Old-fashioned Words
09. Dictionary of Humorous Words
10. Compound Words In English
11. Dictionary of Informal Words
12. Dictionary of Category Words
13. Dictionary of One-word Substitution
14. Hypernyms and Hyponyms
15. Holonyms and Meronyms
16. Oronym Words In English
17. Dictionary of Root Words
18. Dictionary of English Idioms
19. Dictionary of Phrasal Verbs
20. Dictionary of Difficult Words
21. Dictionary of Verbs
22. Dictionary of Adjectives
23. Dictionary of Adverbs
24. Dictionary of Formal Words
25. Dictionary of Technical Words
26. Dictionary of Foreign Words
27. Dictionary of Approving & Disapproving Words
28. Dictionary of Slang Words
29. Advanced English Phrases
30. Words In the English Language

****

(C). SERIES TITLE: "WORDS IN COMMON USAGE" *[10 BOOKS]*

01. How to Use the Word "Break" In English
02. How to Use the Word "Come" In English
03. How to Use the Word "Go" In English
04. How to Use the Word "Have" In English
05. How to Use the Word "Make" In English
06. How to Use the Word "Put" In English
07. How to Use the Word "Run" In English
08. How to Use the Word "Set" In English
09. How to Use the Word "Take" In English
10. How to Use the Word "Turn" In English

****

(D). SERIES TITLE: "WORDS BY NUMBER OF LETTERS" *[10 BOOKS]*

01. Dictionary of 4-Letter Words
02. Dictionary of 5-Letter Words
03. Dictionary of 6-Letter Words
04. Dictionary of 7-Letter Words
05. Dictionary of 8-Letter Words
06. Dictionary of 9-Letter Words
07. Dictionary of 10-Letter Words
08. Dictionary of 11-Letter Words
09. Dictionary of 12- to 14-Letter Words
10. Dictionary of 15- to 18-Letter Words

****

(E). SERIES TITLE: "ENGLISH WORKSHEETS" *[10 BOOKS]*

01. English Word Exercises (Part 1)
02. English Word Exercises (Part 2)
03. English Word Exercises (Part 3)
04. English Sentence Exercises (Part 1)
05. English Sentence Exercises (Part 2)
06. English Sentence Exercises (Part 3)
07. Test Your English
08. Match the Two Parts of the Words
09. Letter-Order In Words
10. Choose the Correct Spelling

Made in the USA
Middletown, DE
03 June 2023

32024082R00044